KT-439-521

Contents

Introduction

'Merry Christmas, Uncle,' said Fred, with a happy smile.
'Bah!' said Scrooge. 'Merry Christmas? Humbug!'

Scrooge is a cold, hard man. He loves money, and he doesn't like people. He really doesn't like Christmas. But then some ghosts visit him. They show him his past, his life now, and a possible future. Will Scrooge learn from the ghosts? Can he change?

Charles Dickens was born in 1812. He wrote *A Christmas Carol* when he was thirty-one. At that time he was famous for other great stories: *Pickwick Papers, Oliver Twist, Nicholas Nickleby* and *The Old Curiosity Shop*. But he had a hard life when he was a child. He never forgot that.

Charles Dickens' father was a clerk in an office, but he lost his money. In Dickens' time, people without any money sometimes went to prison. Young Charles was twelve when his father went to prison. Suddenly, his family was poor. Charles had to leave school and go to work. Later he often wrote about the hard lives of poor people.

In *A Christmas Carol*, Dickens tells us about Christmas in London. In 1843 London was a dirty town. The houses had coal fires, and there was often fog in the streets in winter. But on Christmas Day people sang songs and played games. They went to church, and had goose for Christmas dinner.

Dickens wrote *A Christmas Carol* very quickly, because he wanted it in the shops before Christmas 1843. It was expensive, at twenty-five pence, but 6,000 people bought the book before Christmas.

People will remember Dickens for all his great stories, but they often think of him at Christmas.

Chapter 1   Marley's Ghost

Marley was dead, but the names on the door of the office were Scrooge and Marley. Marley's name was on the door, seven years after he died. And sometimes people called Scrooge 'Scrooge', when they came into the office. And sometimes people called him 'Marley'.

And Scrooge said 'Yes?' when they called him Scrooge. And he answered 'Yes?' when they called him Marley. Scrooge or Marley, it was the same to him.

Scrooge was a hard man, and he loved money. He was a cold man too, a man without any friends. His old face was cold, blue with cold. Cold was with him everywhere. He took it with him, always. He took it to the office of Scrooge and Marley. The office was cold in the summer. But at Christmas time it was colder than the snow outside. And when he left the office, he looked cold too.

Nobody stopped Scrooge in the street and said, 'My dear Scrooge, how are you? When will you come and see me?' People knew him, but poor people didn't ask him for a penny. Children didn't ask him, 'What time is it?' Men and women didn't ask him for help. Dogs knew Scrooge, too. They ran away from him.

Scrooge was happy about all that. He liked it. He didn't want to be with people.

◆

It was Christmas Eve★, and Old Scrooge was busy at his desk. It was very cold. Scrooge could see the people outside in the street.

★ Christmas Eve: 24 December, the day before Christmas Day.

They tried to stay warm but they couldn't. It was only three o'clock but it was dark outside. There were candles in the windows of the other offices near his.

There was a thick fog outside, too. It came into the offices under the doors, and you couldn't see the houses in the same street as Scrooge's office.

Scrooge looked up from his papers. The door of his office was open so he could watch his clerk, Bob Cratchit. The clerk worked in a small room near Scrooge. Scrooge had a very small fire, but the clerk's fire was smaller. He couldn't put coal on it because the coal was in Scrooge's room.

A man came into the office. His name was Fred.

'Merry Christmas, Uncle,' said Fred, with a happy smile.

'Bah!' said Scrooge. 'Merry Christmas? Humbug!'

Fred's face was red from the cold outside. He laughed. And when he laughed, he laughed with his eyes, too. He was cold from outside, but it was colder here in Scrooge's office.

'You don't mean that, Uncle,' he said.

'Yes, I do,' said Scrooge. 'Merry Christmas! Bah! Why are you merry? How can you possibly feel merry? You're too poor for that.'

'Oh!' Fred laughed. 'How can you possibly feel sad? You're too rich for that.'

Scrooge had no better answer, so he said 'Bah!' again. Then he followed it with 'Merry Christmas? Humbug!'

'Don't be angry, Uncle,' said Fred.

'Angry?' said the uncle. 'Yes, I'm angry. I'm angry because I live in a world with happy people in it. Merry Christmas! Why? What's Christmas to you? You want things, but you haven't got the money for them. You're a year older, but not richer. You haven't got as much money as you had last Christmas. People say "Merry Christmas!",' said Scrooge angrily. 'But I think I'd like to eat those people for Christmas dinner!'

'Oh, Uncle!' said Fred, with a smile.

'Young Fred!' said the uncle. 'Have your Christmas. And I'll have mine. Was Christmas good to you, in the past?'

'It was great!' said Fred. 'Christmas is a good time – a kind, happy time. Everybody likes being with people. It's the only time in the year when that happens. And so, Uncle, Christmas was always a good time for me. It didn't make me rich, but it made me happy. And I say "Merry Christmas everybody!"'

'Humbug!' said Scrooge.

'Don't be angry, Uncle. Come and have dinner with us tomorrow, on Christmas Day.'

'No,' said Scrooge. 'And again, no! Good afternoon!'

'But I don't want anything from you. Why can't we be friends?'

'Good afternoon!' said Scrooge.

'So you won't come. I am sorry about that. We were always friends. And because it's Christmas, I want to be a good friend now. So I will say "Merry Christmas", Uncle! And a happy New Year to you!'

'Good afternoon!' said Scrooge.

Fred stopped at the door and said 'Merry Christmas!' to Bob Cratchit, the clerk. Bob was cold, but he answered warmly, 'Merry Christmas to you, sir!'

'There's another stupid person!' said Scrooge. 'My clerk, with only a pound a week for a wife and family, is talking about a merry Christmas!'

The clerk opened the door for Fred and he left. Then two other men in expensive clothes came in. They walked into Scrooge's office and took their hats off. They had books and papers in their hands.

One of the men looked at his papers. 'Scrooge and Marley's, I think?' he said. 'Am I speaking to Mr Scrooge or to Mr Marley?'

'Mr Marley's dead,' answered Scrooge. 'He died on this night, back in 1836.'

'Oh! Dead for seven years, eh?' said the second man. He wrote that down. 'At this happy time of the year, Mr Scrooge, we usually try to do something for the poor people in this city. Things are difficult for them now. Thousands of them are cold. They haven't got any food. Many of them have no home.'

'Aren't there any prisons for them?' asked Scrooge.

'There are a lot of prisons,' the man answered. He put down his pen.

'Aren't there any workhouses for the poor?' asked Scrooge.

'There are,' said the man. 'It's sad, but there are a lot of workhouses.'

'Oh, good. So the prisons and workhouses aren't closed,' said Scrooge coldly. 'I'm happy about that.'

'Prisons and workhouses can't really make people merry at Christmas time,' said the man. 'So we are asking people for money. We will give it to the poor for food and drink. How much will you give us?'

'Nothing!' said Scrooge. '*I'm* not merry at Christmas time and I won't give money to the poor so *they* can be merry. Good afternoon to you!'

The two men looked at Scrooge's hard, unhappy face and left the room.

◆

The fog was thicker now. The night was darker. The cold was colder. It was time to shut the office. Scrooge got up from his chair. Bob Cratchit, the clerk, put out the candle and put on his hat.

'Will you want to be at home all day tomorrow?' asked Scrooge.

'Yes, sir. But are you happy with that?'

'I'm not happy with it, no,' said Scrooge. 'It is not right. I pay you every day when you work. You think that's right. But you also want me to pay you for a day when you don't work.'

The clerk smiled. 'It's only on Christmas Day,' he said.

'Oh, so you can take fifteen pence from me every year and that's all right because it is for the twenty-fifth of December?' said Scrooge. 'Oh, all right. You can have the day at home. Be here early the day after that.'

Scrooge went out, and the clerk shut the office. He ran home as fast as he could. He forgot about work and played with his children.

◆

Scrooge had dinner in a cheap eating-house and then went home. He had rooms in Marley's old house. They were dark and cold. The other rooms in the house were offices now. Only Scrooge lived there.

He opened the door and went in. He lit a candle. Then he walked through his rooms. Was everything in its place? He went into the sitting-room, the bedroom and a little office near the bedroom. His money was in this office. Everything was all right. There was nobody under the table, nobody under the bed. His money was there in the office.

There was a small fire in the sitting-room. He shut the door and sat down by the fire.

He heard the noise of a heavy chain down below. The noise came up the stairs, nearer and nearer his door.

'Humbug!' said Scrooge. 'What *is* that noise?'

Something came through the heavy door and into the room. The little fire suddenly came to life, red and yellow.

It was Marley – Marley in his old clothes. Scrooge knew those clothes well. There was a chain round him – a chain with money on it and money-boxes and money bags.

Scrooge looked at Marley. He could see through him. He could see the back of his coat.

'Well?' said Scrooge, coldly. 'What do you want?'

'A lot!'

5

Scrooge had dinner in a cheap eating-house and then went home.

Yes, it was Marley.

'Who are you?' Scrooge asked. But he knew.

'You mean – who *was* I?

'Who *were* you, then?' said Scrooge.

'In life I was Jacob Marley. Don't you know me?' said the ghost.

'No,' said Scrooge, 'I don't.' But he did.

'Your eyes say it is Marley,' said the ghost. 'Are your eyes wrong?'

'Yes,' said Scrooge. 'My eyes are wrong. Why not? I think I ate something bad. And now I'm seeing you. I think you're bad meat. Not Marley. Humbug!'

The ghost gave a loud cry and made a really loud noise with its chain. Its mouth fell open – it was the mouth of a dead man.

Scrooge fell down on the floor and looked up at the ghost. He put his hands in front of his face.

'Why?' he cried. 'Why are you here? You're dead.'

'Now,' said the ghost, 'do you think I am Jacob Marley? Dead Jacob Marley?'

'I do,' said Scrooge. 'I do! But why are dead people walking the streets, and why does one come to me?'

'It is good,' answered the ghost, 'to be with other people. It is good to be happy when they are happy. It is good to be sad when they are sad. But some people do not do this in life. And what happens to them, do you think?'

'I don't know,' said Scrooge.

'Their *ghosts* walk the streets of the world when they are dead. Their ghosts see happy people but cannot laugh with them. Their ghosts see sad people but cannot cry with them. Their ghosts have to do these things because they did not do them in life.'

Again the ghost gave a cry and moved its chain.

'You've got a chain!' said Scrooge, now very afraid. 'Why? Tell me!'

'I made this chain in my life,' answered the ghost. 'And I am wearing it now. I made it, and I put it on. Do you want to know about *your* chain?'

'My chain?' said Scrooge. 'What chain?'

'You too are making a chain in your life,' said Marley's ghost. 'Your chain was as heavy and as long as this one when I died.'

'What?'

'And in the next seven years you made it heavier and longer.'

'Don't tell me more,' said Scrooge. 'I'm afraid. Make me happier. Talk about something different.'

'I can't,' the ghost answered. 'I can't stay here. I have to go to a new place, always a new place. In life I worked and worked. I was always in the office. I never stopped making money. But now I have to go to many sad places. Always a new place – every day, every minute.'

'Dead for seven years!' thought Scrooge. 'And never in one place!'

'Yes, all the time,' said the ghost. 'I am always moving. Never happy. This time of the year is the worst. Why, in the past, did I turn my eyes away when I walked near people? Why didn't I look at the poor homes? Why didn't I help poor people? Listen to me!'

'I will,' said Scrooge. 'I will! But don't be angry with me!'

'I sat next to you many times in the days after I died.'

This was not a nice thought for Scrooge. 'I am here tonight,' the ghost said, 'because I have to tell you something. I can help you.'

'You were always a good friend to me,' said Scrooge. 'Thank you.'

'Three ghosts will come,' said the ghost of Jacob Marley.

'When?' asked Scrooge.

'The first ghost will come at one o'clock. You will hear the church clock and you will see him. The second ghost will come on the next night at the same time, and the third on the next night at midnight. You will hear midnight on the church clock.'

'And you?' asked Scrooge.

'You won't see me again,' said Marley's ghost, 'but remember my words.'

8

The ghost walked back, away from Scrooge. It walked and the window opened at the same time. When the ghost was at the window, Scrooge heard, from outside, the cries of the sad people in the world. The ghost listened for a minute, and it cried too. And then it went out into the night.

Scrooge went to the window and looked out. There were ghosts outside. They walked up and down the street, and they cried. They all wore a chain.

Scrooge knew some of these ghosts from before, when they were men. They cried because they wanted to help other people. But now they couldn't. Then the ghosts went into the fog and Scrooge couldn't hear them.

The night was quiet again. Scrooge closed the window. He checked the door. He tried to say 'Humbug!' but stopped.

Then he went to bed with his clothes on, and fell asleep.

Chapter 2   The Ghost of Past Christmases

When Scrooge opened his eyes again, it was dark. He looked from his bed, but he couldn't see the window. It was as dark as the walls of the room. He listened. Then he heard the church clock. It was twelve o'clock.

But it was after two when he went to bed. Was the clock wrong? Perhaps the hands of the clock couldn't move because of the snow. Twelve! Twelve?

'It isn't possible!' said Scrooge. 'What happened to a day and most of a night? It's not possible. Can this be twelve midday?'

He got out of bed and went to the window. He looked out. He could only see fog. It was very cold outside. There were no sounds of people in the streets. Was it really midday?

Scrooge went to bed again. He thought about Jacob Marley's ghost. Was he asleep at that time? Then he heard the clock.

'A quarter past twelve,' thought Scrooge.

Later he heard the clock again.

'Half past twelve,' thought Scrooge.

Again. 'A quarter to one,' thought Scrooge. 'A quarter to one!'

And he remembered the words of Marley's ghost. A visit at one o'clock! The first ghost at one o'clock.

He heard the clock. 'One o'clock,' thought Scrooge. 'And . . . and nothing.'

But then a light came into the room. He sat up – and there, at the end of his bed, was a ghost.

The ghost was a child – but also not a child. It was an old man – an old man not bigger than a child. Its long hair was white, old man's hair, but the face was young.

The ghost's clothes were white. It had some Christmas holly in its hand, but there were summer flowers on the clothes. The strangest thing was a white light. It came from the top of the ghost's head. And the ghost had a hat under its arm. Perhaps it put the hat over the light, when it wanted to put out the light.

'Marley said, "Three ghosts will come to you." Are you the first ghost?' asked Scrooge.

'I am,' said the ghost, quietly.

'Who are you and what are you?' asked Scrooge.

'I am the Ghost of Past Christmases.'

'Which past Christmases?' asked Scrooge.

'Yours.'

'Please put on your hat,' said Scrooge.

Scrooge wanted to see the ghost in its hat. But why? He didn't really know the answer to that.

'What?' said the ghost. 'Do you want to put out my light? I am giving this light to you. Your bad past life made this hat. Your bad past life put out the light . . . Come, walk with me!'

The ghost took Scrooge's arm with a strong hand. They went to the window and Scrooge looked down.

'Ghost!' said Scrooge. 'No, I'll fall!'

'No,' the ghost said, 'you won't fall. I am with you.'

◆

They went through the wall of Scrooge's room and stood on an open country road. It was green everywhere. The city was not there now. The dark and the fog were not there. It was a lovely cold winter day with snow on the ground.

Scrooge looked round with wide eyes.

'I . . .' he said, 'I was born here. I was a boy here.'

'Do you remember the way?' asked the ghost.

'Remember it?' cried Scrooge. 'I can close my eyes and walk there!'

'Then why did you forget it for so many years?' said the ghost.

'Let's go.'

They walked down the road. Scrooge knew every tree. Then they saw a little town with its bridge, its church and the river.

Scrooge saw some boys on horses. They called to other boys. They all shouted happily. People laughed when they heard them.

'These are ghosts from the past,' said the Ghost of Past Christmases. 'They can't see us.'

But Scrooge and the ghost were happy to see the children. And Scrooge knew every ghost. These people said 'Merry Christmas' to their friends. Then they said 'Goodbye' and went home.

'They were at school,' said the ghost. 'And there is one child at the school now, when the other children are at home – a child without any friends.'

'Yes,' said Scrooge. 'I know! I know!' And he began to cry.

They walked again – Scrooge knew the street well. Then they stopped when they came to a large red house. There was nobody there. A rich man built the house but then he lost all his money. There weren't any doors or windows in the house now.

Scrooge and the ghost went into the house. They saw a long,

11

It was a lovely cold winter day with snow on the ground.

ugly room with desks in it. A boy sat at one of the desks and read.

Scrooge sat down next to the boy – it was young Scrooge. He cried when he saw his past.

The boy read and Scrooge watched. He knew the book well.

'Oh, it's Ali Baba!' he cried. 'Dear old Ali Baba! Yes, I remember.'

One Christmas time, when his mother and father weren't at home, Ali Baba came to him in his story book. Ah, yes, and other people from stories: Robinson Crusoe ran by the sea with Man Friday . . .

'Sad, sad boy!' said Scrooge. 'I want to give. . . Oh! But it's too late now.'

'What do you mean?' asked the ghost.

'Nothing,' said Scrooge, 'nothing. . . There was a boy at my door last night. He sang a Christmas carol for me. But I didn't give him any money, and I can't do it now.'

The ghost smiled. 'Let's see another Christmas,' it said.

◆

The school-room was darker now. There was young Scrooge at his desk, when the other boys were on holiday. Then he stopped reading and started walking sadly up and down the room.

The door opened, and a little girl came in. She was younger than the boy. She put her arms round him. Then she said, 'Dear, dear brother. I am here because you can come home now.'

'Home, little Fan?' said the boy.

'Yes,' said the child, happily, 'home for always. Father is kinder now. He spoke kindly to me one night before I went to bed. Then I was not afraid. I asked him again, "Can Ebenezer come home?"'

'What did he say?' asked the boy – young Scrooge. 'What did Father say?'

'He said "Yes". And he sent me and I'm bringing you home! We'll be a family this Christmas and we'll have the happiest time in the world.'

'You are a good woman, little Fan,' said Ebenezer Scrooge.

She laughed and tried to put her hand up to his face. But she was too small and she couldn't do it. So she laughed again.

'Dear little Fan!' said Scrooge, the man. 'She was very small, and not very strong.'

'Very small,' said the ghost, 'but very kind too. She died when she was a young woman. She had children, I think.'

'One child,' said Scrooge.

'Yes, one child,' said the ghost. 'His name is Fred.'

'Yes,' said Scrooge, quietly. 'Fan's boy, Fred.'

◆

They left the school and walked outside again. Scrooge looked round. They were now in a busy street in the city. The ghost stopped at the door of a big office.

'Do you know this place?' it asked.

'Know it?' said Scrooge. 'Yes! I started work here!'

They went in. An old man sat behind a high desk.

'It's old Fezziwig, the dear old man! It's Fezziwig, and he isn't dead now!'

Old Fezziwig put down his pen and looked up at the clock. It was seven o'clock. He laughed and called merrily, 'Ho there! Ebenezer! Dick!'

Scrooge in his past life, now a young man, came in. With him was the other clerk, Dick.

'Dick Wilkins!' said Scrooge to the ghost. 'Yes, there he is! He was a great friend, old Dick!'

'Come, my boys,' said Fezziwig. 'Stop work now! It's Christmas Eve. Let's shut the office and put the desks and chairs by the wall. Let's have a party.'

They pushed the desks and chairs to the wall. They lit more candles and put more coal on the fire.

Mrs Fezziwig came in with the three lovely Miss Fezziwigs, and behind the Miss Fezziwigs came three young men. Each man was, of course, in love with one Miss Fezziwig. Then more young men and women came in. They worked in the office.

There was music, and the dancing began. There was cake and meat and wine.

The party finished at eleven o'clock. Mr and Mrs Fezziwig stood at the door and said 'Goodbye!' to everybody. 'Merry Christmas!' they called. 'Merry Christmas!'

Scrooge watched his past life. He remembered everything and enjoyed everything. He was very excited. The young Ebenezer Scrooge was, he thought, a very nice young man.

Now, at the end of the party, he remembered the ghost. The ghost looked at him. The light on its head shone yellow.

'The party was a small thing,' said the ghost, 'but it made those unimportant people very happy.'

'A small thing!' said Scrooge. 'No!'

'Listen to the two young men,' the ghost said.

The two young men stood outside Fezziwig's office in the dark and talked about Fezziwig.

One of them said, 'He's a fine man.'

'*Was* Fezziwig really wonderful?' the ghost asked Scrooge. 'What do you think? The party cost a little money – not much.'

'Oh no! It was more important than that,' said Scrooge. 'Fezziwig could make us happy or unhappy. He could make our work light or heavy. He could make our lives good or bad with a word or with a look. He made us happy in small ways, and with small things – but with a lot of small things. You can't buy those small things – not with all the money in the world. You. . .'

The ghost looked hard at him and he stopped.

'What is it?' asked the ghost.

Scrooge said nothing for a minute. And then he said, 'I want to say a word or two to Dick Wilkins.'

But Dick Wilkins said goodbye to his friend, the younger Scrooge, and went home.

Scrooge and the ghost stood outside the office in the dark.

'My time here is nearly at an end,' said the ghost. 'Quickly!'

◆

Again, Scrooge saw Ebenezer Scrooge in the past. But he was older now. He was very different. His eyes said, 'Where's the money, where's the money?' Money was his life now.

Scrooge sat with a young girl. The girl cried and Scrooge watched her. 'No,' said the girl, quietly. 'You have a new love now. I hope you will be happy with your new love in the future.'

'What love?' he asked her.

'The love of money. You are a different man now, because you have the love of money in your life.'

He wanted to speak but she didn't look at him. She said, 'I am leaving now. I hope you and your money will be happy.' And she left.

'Ghost!' cried Scrooge. 'Don't show me more! Take me home!'

But the ghost said, 'You have to see in your past one more time, Ebenezer Scrooge!'

◆

They were in another place, a small but beautiful room. Near the fire there was a lovely young girl, and opposite her sat her mother. The mother was the woman from Scrooge's past. He loved her and then lost her.

There was a great noise in the room. There were a lot of very happy, very noisy children. The mother and daughter looked happy too. Then the door opened and the father came in. He had Christmas boxes in his arms. Everybody opened a box, and shouted happily.

Later the younger children climbed up the stairs to the top of the house and went to bed. The man sat down by the fire with his daughter and her mother.

The husband turned to his wife with a smile. 'I saw your old friend this afternoon.'

'Which old friend?'

'Who do you think?'

'I don't know!' And then she asked, 'Was it Ebenezer Scrooge?'

'Yes,' he said, 'it was Mr Scrooge. I looked in his office window. I saw him by the light of a candle. Mr Marley is dying, I hear. And there Scrooge sat without a friend in the world.'

'Ghost!' cried Scrooge sadly. 'Take me home!'

'These are the ghosts of your past,' said the ghost. 'They are your life. What did you do with your life?'

'Leave me! Take me home!'

Scrooge took the ghost's hat and put it on the ghost's head. The light went out. Scrooge was in his bedroom at home again. He went to bed and cried. He only stopped crying when sleep came.

Chapter 3   The Ghost of Christmas Now

Scrooge woke up and sat up in bed. He heard the church clock. Yes, it was time for the second ghost. It was one o'clock. He wanted to see the ghost when it arrived. He didn't want it to come up behind him. But there wasn't a ghost in the room.

He waited. Five minutes . . . Ten minutes . . . Then, from his bed, he saw a red light in the next room. What was it?

He got up and put on his shoes. Then he went to the door. When he opened the door, somebody or something called him by his name.

He looked into the room. It was *his* room, but very different. The walls had green holly on them. There was a big fire, and on the floor was lovely Christmas food – a Christmas goose, fruit, cakes, bottles of wine.

'Come in,' said the ghost. 'Come in! Look! Here I am!'

Scrooge went into the room and stood in front of the ghost. This was not the hard Scrooge from the past. He could not look the ghost in the eye. He looked at the floor.

'I am the Ghost of Christmas Now,' said the ghost. 'Look at me!'

Scrooge looked. He saw a fat, merry person in a long green coat. It had no shoes on its feet but it had holly on its head in its long brown hair.

'I'm different from everybody in your life,' said the ghost.

'Oh yes,' said Scrooge. 'Ghost, take me with you. Last night I went with the other ghost and I learned a lesson. Tonight you can teach me and I will learn.'

'Give me your hand.'

◆

The Christmas goose, fruit, cakes and bottles of wine weren't there now. The room and the fire weren't there. Scrooge and the Ghost of Christmas Now were in a city street.

It was Christmas morning. There was snow in the road in front of the houses. The sky was grey, but the people were happy. They were outside their houses in the snow. They shouted merrily and threw snowballs. They laughed when a snowball hit them.

Then the people stopped playing in the snow and listened to the church clock. Time for church! Everybody went inside, but they were quickly out in the street again in their best clothes, with happy faces.

These people couldn't see Scrooge and the ghost. Scrooge and the ghost walked a long way through the streets to the house of Bob Cratchit, Scrooge's clerk.

Inside the house was Mrs Cratchit, in her best clothes. She made dinner, and Belinda, her daughter, helped her. Peter Cratchit, her

He saw a fat, merry person in a long green coat.

son, watched some food on the fire and two smaller Cratchits, a boy and a girl, danced round and round the table.

'Where's your father?' asked Mrs Cratchit. 'And where's your brother, Tiny Tim?'

Tiny Tim was the youngest child. He was very small for his age.

'And where's Martha?' asked Mrs Cratchit. 'She wasn't as late as this last Christmas.'

'Here I am, Mother,' said a girl. She came in through the door.

'Here's Martha, Mother!' cried the two young Cratchits.

'Martha, you're very late!' said Mrs Cratchit. She smiled at her oldest daughter and took her hat and coat.

'We had to do a lot of work in the shop last night,' answered the girl, 'and we had to finish it this morning.'

'Well, all right. You're here now!' said Mrs Cratchit. 'Sit down by the fire and get warm.'

The two young Cratchits ran and played. 'Father's coming!' called one of them. 'Stand behind the door, Martha, so Father can't see you!'

So Martha stood behind the door. Then Bob Cratchit, her father, came in. His clothes were old but very clean. Bob had Tiny Tim on his back. Tiny Tim could not walk without help.

'Where's our Martha?' said Bob Cratchit. He looked round the room.

'She isn't coming,' said Mrs Cratchit.

'She isn't coming!' said Bob Cratchit. 'She isn't coming on Christmas Day?'

Martha could not stay behind the door now. She didn't want him to be unhappy, not for a minute. So she ran to him and put her arms round him.

The two young Cratchits took Tiny Tim away. They watched the dinner on the kitchen fire.

'How was Tiny Tim in church?' asked Mrs Cratchit.

'He was very good,' said Bob. 'I think that he's a little stronger.'

Tiny Tim's brother and sister helped Tiny Tim to his little chair by the fire. Bob Cratchit put some fruit in the wine and made a wonderful Christmas drink. He put it down by the fire.

When the dinner was ready, Bob Cratchit put Tiny Tim in his little chair near him at the table. Then Mrs Cratchit brought in the goose, and the family watched with open eyes. The family ate it – all of it.

Bob Cratchit said, 'That's the best goose in the world!'

Everybody said, 'Yes! It's the best goose in the world.'

It was really not a very big goose. But nobody said that – and nobody thought it. The Cratchits had very little money and for them the goose was wonderful.

After dinner the family sat round the fire and enjoyed Bob Cratchit's drink, the hot wine with fruit in it.

Bob Cratchit stood up and said, 'Let's drink to a merry Christmas to us all. Merry Christmas!'

And everybody said, 'A Merry Christmas to us all!'

'Merry Christmas!' said Tiny Tim.

He sat very close to his father on his little chair, and Bob Cratchit put his hand over his tiny one. He loved the child and wanted him near him. But he was afraid. The boy was very ill.

'Ghost,' said Scrooge. 'Please tell me something. Will Tiny Tim live?'

'I can see Tiny Tim's chair,' answered the ghost. 'It is near the fire. Nobody is sitting on it. These are only ghosts of the future. They are possible, only possible. But in this future, the child will die.'

'No, no!' said Scrooge. 'Oh, no, kind ghost! Say that he will live!'

'In this future the Ghost of Future Christmases will not find him here. But is that important? You often say, "There are too many people in the world."'

◆

Bob Cratchit stood up again, and he said, 'Mr Scrooge! Let's drink to Mr Scrooge!'

'I want to talk to Mr Scrooge,' said Mrs Cratchit. 'I want to say something to him. And he won't eat a Christmas dinner when he hears it!'

'Oh no!' said Bob Cratchit. 'Remember the children! This is Christmas Day.'

'And you can only drink to a cold money-lover on Christmas Day,' said Mrs Cratchit. You know Mr Scrooge, Robert. Nobody knows him better than you.'

'Oh no!' said Bob. 'This is Christmas Day.'

'Well,' said Mrs Cratchit, 'I'll drink to him because you ask me. I hope he has a merry Christmas and a happy New Year. But I don't think he will!'

Mr Scrooge's name made the party sad, but five minutes later they were all happy again. There was work for Peter, Bob Cratchit told them, in an office near him. The two young Cratchits laughed at the idea of Peter in an office.

Martha began to talk about her work in the dressmaker's shop. She told them some stories about life in the shop.

She said, 'Tomorrow I'll stay in bed all morning for a good, long sleep.'

They drank more hot drink and then they sang some songs. There was one song about a child in the snow, without his mother and father. Tiny Tim sang it beautifully.

◆

The ghost and Scrooge went through the dark night to the next place. They were in a light room. Scrooge heard a happy laugh. It was Fred's laugh.

'Ha, ha!' laughed Fred. 'Ha, ha, ha!'

When Fred laughed loudly, his wife always laughed too. Then their friends had to laugh.

'My uncle, Ebenezer Scrooge, says "Humbug!" when you say "Merry Christmas" to him. He does it every time!'

'That's very bad,' said his wife. Fred's wife was very pretty. She had a dear little mouth and lovely big brown eyes.

'My uncle is a very funny man,' said Fred. 'I mean it! He's not nice, but he's very unhappy. So I try to be kind to him.'

'He's very rich, Fred,' said his wife. 'You're always telling me he's rich.'

'Well, that doesn't help him, my dear. He doesn't buy anything with it – he lives the life of a poor man. He doesn't help people with it. He doesn't think, "Ah, I'll help that nice Fred and his pretty wife with my money!" – ha-ha-ha! –'

'He makes me angry,' said his wife. His wife's sisters and the other women said the same.

'Oh, I'm sorry for him,' said Fred. 'I couldn't be angry with him. Who's unhappy because Scrooge is hard and cold? Scrooge is. Only him.'

'What do you mean?' asked his wife.

'He doesn't like us', said Fred. 'So he doesn't come and have dinner with us. Who loses? Scrooge loses. He loses a dinner – a very good dinner. But I want to ask him for Christmas dinner again next year, because I'm sorry for him.'

◆

Fred and his friends sat round the fire and sang. After that, they played games. Scrooge was very interested in the games and he wanted to play too.

Then they started to play a new game. It was called "Yes and No". Fred had to think of something and the others had to ask questions about it. Fred could only answer their questions with 'yes' or 'no'.

'Is it an animal?'

'Yes.'

'A nice animal?'

'No.'

'Can you find it in London?'

'Yes.'

'Do you see it in the streets?'

'Yes.'

'Do people pay before they see it?'

'No.'

'Do people eat it?'

'No.'

'Is it a horse?'

'No.'

'Is it a dog?'

'No.'

'Is it a cat?'

'No.'

Fred answered the questions, and he laughed all the time. Everybody laughed, but Fred's wife's sister was the loudest.

'I know!' she cried. 'Fred, I know the answer!'

'What is it?' asked Fred.

'It's your Uncle Scrooge!'

And it was.

'Let's drink to Uncle Scrooge!' said Fred.

They took their glasses in their hands.

'Uncle Scrooge!' they cried.

'A Merry Christmas and a Happy New Year to the old man!' said Fred.

Scrooge wanted to say thank you to them, but the ghost didn't give him time.

He and the ghost went to many other places. They went to other countries, to the homes of rich people and the homes of poor people, to hospitals and to prisons. And everywhere, the ghost wanted to help people.

It was a long night, and the ghost looked older and older. Its hair was now grey.

'Are ghosts' lives very short?' Scrooge asked.

'My life in this world is very short,' answered the ghost. 'It ends tonight.'

'Tonight?' cried Scrooge.

'Yes, tonight at midnight. Listen! It's nearly time.'

It was a quarter to twelve. They could hear the church clock.

'Can I ask you something?' said Scrooge. 'What are those strange things, next to you?'

The ghost showed him two children, a boy and a girl. They were children but their faces weren't young. Their faces were thin and their eyes were the eyes of hungry animals. Their clothes were very old.

The two children sat down at the ghost's feet.

'Ghost,' said Scrooge, 'are they yours?'

'They are Everybody's,' said the ghost. It looked down at the children.

'I don't understand,' said Scrooge.

'This boy could not go to school,' said the ghost. 'The family was too poor – it was not possible. So he learned nothing and he knows nothing. And he will always know nothing.'

'And the girl?' asked Scrooge.

'This girl is hungry,' said the ghost. 'There is no food for her.'

'Can't somebody help them?' cried Scrooge. 'Isn't there a place for them somewhere?'

'Aren't there any prisons?' said the ghost. 'Aren't there any workhouses?'

They were Scrooge's words.

It was twelve. They heard it on the church clock. Scrooge looked for the ghost but couldn't see it.

Then he remembered Marley's words and he saw a grey ghost. It came nearer and nearer to him through the fog.

Chapter 4   The Ghost of Future Christmases

The ghost was in black clothes. Scrooge couldn't see its face – only one hand in the dark night. But the ghost was tall, he thought. He was afraid of it. It came near him. But it didn't speak and it didn't move.

'Are you the Ghost of Future Christmases?' asked Scrooge.

The ghost didn't answer, but its hand moved. The answer was 'yes.'

'You're going to show me the ghosts of possible futures,' said Scrooge. 'I'm afraid of you. I'm more afraid than I was with the other two ghosts. But I know that you want to help me. I hope I'll be a different man in the future. So I'll happily go with you. Why don't you speak?'

The ghost didn't say anything, but its hand was in front of them.

'I'll follow,' said Scrooge.

◆

They left the busy centre of the city. The ghost took Scrooge to some poor streets. They were small and dirty, with small ugly shops and houses. It was a sad place. These streets were new to him, but he knew their names. Everybody knew their names – they were the worst and poorest streets in the city.

Scrooge and the ghost came to a shop. Very poor people brought things to this shop when they wanted to sell them. A man of about seventy, with grey hair, sat by a small fire in the room behind the shop.

When Scrooge and the ghost came into the shop, two women came in too. The women had heavy bags. One of them cleaned people's houses and the other washed their clothes. Then a man in black arrived. He was an undertaker's man.

They all laughed.

'The cleaner can be first,' said the washerwoman. 'Then me second and this man third.'

'Right,' said old Joe, the man with grey hair, 'come inside. I'll shut the door of my shop. Come into the back room.'

The washerwoman threw her bag on the floor of the back room and looked at the other two.

'So, Mrs Dilber,' she said. 'The important thing is – what can *I* get from it? He always asked that question.'

'That's right,' said Mrs Dilber, the cleaner. 'Nobody asked that question more than him.'

'Then who will know that we took one or two things? We can take things. Why not?'

'Yes, why not?' said Mrs Dilber.

'Why not?' said the undertaker's man.

'He's dead. He can't use these things,' the washerwoman said.

'That's right,' said Mrs Dilber and she laughed. 'You can't use things when you're dead.'

'No, you can't take your things with you. And you can't give them to anybody when there's nobody there. There was nobody there when *he* died,' said the undertaker's man.

'Oh, that's right,' said Mrs Dilber. 'Of course there was nobody there. And I'm happy about that. He was never there for anybody.'

'Oh, yes! Now, open the bag, old Joe,' said the washerwoman. 'These are his things. How much money can I have for them?'

Mrs Dilber wanted to be first, but in the end the undertaker's man showed old Joe his things. Old Joe looked at everything and wrote it down.

'There you are,' he said to the undertaker's man. And he showed him the paper. 'I'll give you this for it. I won't give you a penny more than that. Now, who's next?'

The washerwoman was next. She had some clothes, but she also had some books.

'I always give too much to women,' said old Joe. 'There you are. But don't ask me for another penny.'

'Now look at mine,' said the cleaner. Joe opened the cleaner's bag.

'What are these?' he said. 'Bed curtains?'

'Yes,' said the cleaner, and she laughed. 'Bed curtains.'

'Did you really take them when he was on the bed?' asked Joe.

'Yes, that's right,' said Mrs Dilber. 'Why not? And those are his bedclothes.'

'His bedclothes?' said Joe.

'Yes. And there's his night-shirt. I took it from him when he was on the bed. I wasn't afraid of him, because he was dead at the time. We were all afraid of him before he was dead – but not after. Ha-ha-ha!'

◆

'Ghost,' said Scrooge. 'I understand. This was an unhappy man with an unhappy life. My life is the same. But oh! What's this?'

He was next to a bed with no curtains. On it was a man. The man was dead now. But before he died, nobody loved him.

The ghost showed Scrooge the head. It was dark in the room and Scrooge couldn't see the face. And he didn't want to see it!

He looked at the bed and thought, 'A love of money finished this man. Here he is, dead on his bed. And there is nobody here – not a man, woman or child. Nobody thought, "He was kind to me, so I will be kind to him." '

'Ghost,' he said, 'this is a strange, sad place. I am learning its lesson. Let's go.'

But again the ghost showed him the head of the man on the bed.

'I understand you,' said Scrooge, 'but I don't want to see the face.'

The ghost looked at him.

Scrooge spoke again, 'Is anybody in this town sad because this man is dead?' he asked. 'Show me somebody, ghost, please.'

◆

The ghost moved its arm – and they were in a room. It was daytime and a mother and child were there.

The mother looked out of the window, then looked at the clock. She waited and hoped. Then she heard a noise outside the door. She went to the door quickly and met her husband. He was young but now his face was sad.

'Well?' she asked. 'Is it good or bad?'

'Bad,' he answered.

'Then we have no hope?'

'No, there is some hope, Caroline.'

'He can be kind to us,' she said, 'so there is hope.'

'He can't be kind to us,' said her husband. 'Not now. He's dead. You know I tried to see him. I wanted to ask him for one more week. One more week and then we can pay. But he was very ill – his cleaner told me. He died later.'

'So who do we give the money to? Who will we have to pay?'

'I don't know. But we'll have the money next week, and nobody can be worse than him. We can sleep well tonight, Caroline.'

'Ghost! I want to see a *sad* person. Is everybody always happy when somebody dies?' cried Scrooge.

◆

The ghost took him to a different street. Scrooge knew that street well. They went into Bob Cratchit's house. The mother and children were there round the fire.

It was quiet – very quiet. The little Cratchits looked at Peter. Peter read to them very quietly.

And then the mother and daughters started cooking, but they were very quiet too. The mother put some food on the table.

'He'll be here in a minute,' she said.

'I think he walks very slowly these days,' answered Peter, and he closed the book. 'He often walked very fast with Tiny Tim on his back...'

'Tiny Tim was very light,' said the mother, 'and his father loved him so much!...There's your father at the door now.'

She ran out to him.

'Did you visit Tiny Tim's grave today, Bob?' she asked.

'Yes, my dear. It's in a green place. But you'll see it often. We'll walk there every Sunday. I told Tiny Tim before he died. My dear little child!' cried Bob.

Then the girls and their mother went back to their cooking. Bob told them more about his visit to Tiny Tim's grave.

'I met Fred in the street. "Why are you sad?" he asked, and I told him. "I'm very sorry about that, Mr Cratchit," he said, "and very sorry for your good wife. I want to help," he said. "You know my address. Please come and see me." Fred never knew Tiny Tim, but he was unhappy too.'

'I know he's a very good man,' said Mrs Cratchit.

'Yes,' answered Bob, 'and he's going to try to get a better job for Peter.'

◆

'Ghost,' said Scrooge, 'I think you're going to leave me in a short time. Tell me one thing: Who was the dead man?'

The ghost said nothing. But it walked, and Scrooge followed. They went to a church, and in front of the church there were some graves. The ghost stood next to one.

'Answer me one question,' said Scrooge. 'Are these really the ghosts of the future, or are you only showing me a *possible* future?'

Again, the ghost did not answer. He looked down at the grave at his feet.

'People do things and then other things happen,' said Scrooge. 'But the same people can do different things and then different things will happen in the future. Isn't that right? We can change the future.'

The ghost did not move. Scrooge read the name on the grave. It was EBENEZER SCROOGE.

'Ghost!' cried Scrooge. 'I won't forget the lessons of the three ghosts. I'll learn from the past, from now and from the possible future. I'll be kind at Christmas. I'll be kind all year. And then my future will be different from my past! I'll change my future!'

Chapter 5   The End of the Story

Ebenezer Scrooge was in his room again.

'I'll be kind at Christmas and all year,' he said again. He climbed out of bed. 'The three ghosts will help me.'

He looked at his bed curtains.

'The bed curtains are there,' he thought. 'The bed curtains are there and I'm here. That future, the future with the two women and the undertaker's man – it didn't happen!'

He went into another room.

'There's the door,' he said. 'Marley's ghost came in through that door. And the Ghost of Christmas Now sat there, and that's the window. I saw the Ghost of Future Christmases at that window. It all happened! Ha-ha-ha!'

This was Ebenezer's first laugh for many years. The first laugh of a new future.

'What day is it?' thought Ebenezer. 'How much time did I have with the ghosts? I don't know.'

He heard the church clock. He ran to the window and opened it. There was no fog, only sun.

'What's today?' called Ebenezer to a boy in the street. The boy was in his best clothes.

Scrooge read the name on the grave.

'Eh?' said the boy.

'What's today?' said Ebenezer.

'Today?' answered the boy. 'It's Christmas Day, of course!'

'It's Christmas Day!' said Ebenezer. 'It's *my* Christmas Day! I was with the ghosts for one night. Only one night! Hello, my boy! Do you know that shop in the next street? There was a big goose in the window. A *very* big goose!'

'Was it as big as me?' asked the boy.

'Yes, my boy,' said Scrooge.

'It's in the window now,' said the boy.

'Is it?' said Scrooge. 'Well, go and buy it. The man can bring it here. Come back with him, and I'll give you ten pence. Come back in five minutes, and I'll give you twenty pence.'

The boy ran to the shop.

'I'll send the goose to Bob Cratchit's house,' Ebenezer thought. 'But not from me. I won't put my name on it. That goose is bigger than Tiny Tim!'

Ebenezer went to his bedroom and put on his best clothes. The man arrived with the goose. Ebenezer paid him and the boy. He gave the man Bob Cratchit's address, and then he went out into the streets. People started to come out of their houses. Ebenezer remembered them from his time with the Ghost of Christmas Now.

Ebenezer walked with his hands behind him and looked at them with a big smile. Because he looked happy, three or four men said, 'Good morning, sir. A Merry Christmas to you!' That 'Merry Christmas' was the happiest sound in his life.

Then he saw somebody.

'I know that man,' thought Ebenezer. 'Sir, you were in my office yesterday,' he said. 'You said "Scrooge and Marley's, I think? Am I speaking to Mr Scrooge or to Mr Marley?" Do you remember?'

'Yes,' said the man, 'that's right.'

'My dear sir,' said Ebenezer, and he took the man's hand, 'how do you do? I hope you got a lot of money yesterday. A Merry Christmas to you, sir!'

'Mr Scrooge?' said the man. 'Is that you?'

'Yes,' said Ebenezer. 'That's my name. I know you don't like the sound of it. But I'm a new man now. Will you please. . .' Scrooge spoke very quietly.

'Oh!' said the man. 'My dear Mr Scrooge, do you mean it?'

'Oh yes!' said Ebenezer. 'Please, I want to give you that – every penny. And I'll give you more. Come to my office and I'll give you the money.'

'I will!' said the man.

Ebenezer went to church and then walked through the streets and watched people.

In the afternoon, he went to Fred's house. But he was afraid. He looked at the door for a long time before he went in. A girl came to the door.

'Is Fred at home?' he asked.

'Yes, sir.'

'Where is he, my dear?' said Ebenezer.

'He's in the dining-room, sir.'

'Thank you. He knows me. I'll go in,' said Scrooge.

They were all at the table, and the food was in front of them.

'Fred!' said Ebenezer.

'Well, well, well!' cried Fred. 'Who's this?'

'It's your Uncle Ebenezer. I'm here for dinner. Can I come in, Fred?'

It was a wonderful party with lovely food and games, and everybody was very, very happy.

◆

Ebenezer was early at the office next morning. It was nine o'clock, but Bob Cratchit wasn't there. A quarter past nine – and

Ebenezer walked through the streets and watched people.

no Bob Cratchit. He was eighteen minutes late. Scrooge sat there with the door open. He wanted to see Bob when he arrived.

Then Bob came in.

'Hello,' said Scrooge – the old Scrooge spoke. 'Why are you late?'

'I'm sorry, sir,' said Bob. 'I am late, that's right. I had a very Merry Christmas yesterday.'

'Well,' said Ebenezer, 'I'm going to do something. I'm going to give you more money. And I'll help you with your family. We'll talk about that this afternoon. Now please put more coal on the fire. And you can take some coal into your room, Bob Cratchit.'

◆

Tiny Tim did not die. Ebenezer Scrooge was a second father to the family. He was a good man and a good friend. He always had a good time at Christmas, and he never said 'Humbug!' again.

ACTIVITIES

Chapter 1

Before you read

1 This book is from 1843. Christmas Day was a holiday for most people. What happened on that day, do you think?

2 Find these words in your dictionary. They are all in the story. Use them in the sentences.

candle chain clerk coal fog ghost humbug merry past poor prison workhouse

a '..... Christmas!'

b In the ....., people with no money had to live in a ..... .

c There was no light, so I used a ..... .

d We can't see anything through the ..... .

e Please put some ..... on the fire.

f Why are you afraid? Did you see a .....?

g ..... people can't buy expensive food for Christmas.

h He is a ..... in a small office.

i She killed a man and went to ..... .

j They pulled the ....., and the car came out of the river.

3 Read these sentences. Which person doesn't like Christmas, do you think?

A: 'Christmas is wonderful!'

B: 'Humbug!'

After you read

4 Who thought these things?

a 'It's cold here, but Mr Scrooge has got the coal.'

b 'Why is my rich uncle always unhappy?'

c 'Let's go. Scrooge won't give us any money.'

d 'Scrooge's chain is heavier and longer than mine.'

e 'Three ghosts are going to come. What will they say?'

Chapters 2–3

Before you read

5 What do you think the ghosts *will* say?

6 Answer the questions. Find the words in *italics* in your dictionary.
  a Do you sing a *carol* or eat it?   c Can a *goose* fly?
  b What colour is *holly*?   d Is a *tiny* child large?

After you read

7 Who or what:
  a has a light above its head?
  b had no friends?
  c was little Fan?
  d was Mr Fezziwig?
  e was more important to Scrooge than a girl's love?
  f is small, weak and ill?
  g feels sorry for Scrooge?

8 Would you like to work for Mr Fezziwig or for Scrooge? Why?

9 How do you play the 'Yes and No' game? Play it with other students.

Chapters 4–5

Before you read

10 What do you think will happen in the end? Finish these sentences.
  a In a possible future, Scrooge sees a dead man. Nobody is unhappy. The man is. . .
  b In a possible future another person dies. Everybody is unhappy. This person is. . .
  c At the end of the story, Scrooge. . .

11 Find these words in your dictionary. Which are words for people? Where do you find the other things?
   curtain   grave   undertaker   washerwoman

After you read

12 Look at these sentences. Are they about Scrooge before or after the ghosts came to him?

    a People and dogs did not want to be near him.

    b He bought a big goose for Bob Cratchit's family.

    c He did not want Bob to have a day's holiday at Christmas.

    d He lost a lovely woman because he loved money more.

    e He had no friends at school.

    f He did not like Christmas games.

    g He was a second father to the Cratchit children.

Writing

13 Write about Ebenezer Scrooge before and after the ghosts came to him. You can use a–g above, but write other sentences too.

14 Which person (or ghost) in the story do you like best? Why? Write about them.

15 You are Bob Cratchit. You know now that Scrooge gave you the big goose. Write a letter to him and say thank you.

16 What will happen when Scrooge dies? Write about that day.

Answers for the Activities in this book are published in our free resource packs for teachers, the Penguin Readers Factsheets, or available on a separate sheet. Please write to your local Pearson Education office or to: Marketing Department, Penguin Longman Publishing, 5 Bentinck Street, London W1M 5RN.